VICTORIOUS LIVING

Copyright © 2018 Stella Jack.

All rights reserved. First paperback edition printed 2018 in the United Kingdom a

catalogue record for this book is available

from the British Library.

ISBN **978-1-9164071-1-4**

No part of this book shall be reproduced or transmitted in any form or by any means, electronic or mechanical, including photocopying, recording, or by any information retrieval system without written permission of the publisher.

Published by Scribblecity Publications.

Printed in Great Britain

Although every precaution has been taken in

the preparation of this book, the publisher and author assume no responsibility for errors or omissions. Neither is any liability assumed for damages resulting from the use of this information contained herein.

Dedication

To all whose lives have been touched by my teaching ministry, I dedicate this book. Aside from my desire to know God through his word, you continue to motivate me to search for truth in the Word of God. I enjoy taking this journey of discovery with you into God's abundant life.

CONTENTS

Introduction 7

The Battlefield of the Mind 9

Pray 48

The Purpose of Trials and Troubles 60

According to Your Faith 78

Learn From Israel 83

Introduction

It is refreshing to discover that I am the architect of my own destiny. It is not in Satan's hand because he was defeated when Jesus died and rose from the grave. Satan has lost the legal hold over my life. My destiny should not be shaped by my background or family lineage because when I received Christ, I became engrafted into God's kingdom and family lineage.

My destiny should not be limited by my age because at all ages, men have been world changers. Moses became a deliverer at 80 years. This was after he spent 40 years in the wilderness. Josiah was anointed king, and began to reign at 7 years.

It should not be limited by my female gender, because God used several women to change the world. Esther was used to save the Jewish nation, and Mary was used to birth the Messiah.

My destiny is shaped by the image I have in my mind about myself and my relationship with God. God is limited by the image I have about who I am and what he desires to do through me.

As you read, you will discover many truths that will set you free and launch you into a new relationship with your heavenly father.

Chapter 1

The Battlefield of the Mind

Ephesians 6:11-17

¹¹ Put on the full armor of God, so that you can take your stand against the devil's schemes. ¹² For our struggle is not against flesh and blood, but against the rulers, against the authorities, against the powers of this dark world and against the spiritual forces of evil in the heavenly realms. ¹³ Therefore put on the full armor of God, so that when the day of evil comes, you may be able to stand your ground, and after you have done everything, to stand. ¹⁴ Stand firm then, with the belt of truth buckled around your waist, with the breastplate of righteousness in place, ¹⁵ and with your feet fitted with the readiness that comes from the gospel of peace. ¹⁶ In addition to all this, take up the shield of faith, with which you can extinguish all the flaming arrows of the evil one. ¹⁷ Take the helmet of

salvation and the sword of the Spirit, which is the word of God.

Have you ever heard of believers who say they are fighting spiritual warfare? They claim that there are forces of darkness that need to be defeated because they block prayers from getting to heaven where God dwells. These forces of darkness are territorial demons. They claim that except those demons are dealt with, the gospel and prayers will be hindered. This warfare is sometimes called spiritual mapping. Years ago, I thought in the same way, and even joined to carry out such "spiritual battles." This was because I didn't grasp the nature of the warfare we are in. I wondered why some people say we are not fighting demons. Another person went further to say that the Bible never asked us to bind demons. However, look closely at these scriptures, and you will see that although our enemy is the devil and his forces, our warfare is not against them, because they have been defeated by Jesus on the cross. A study of the New Testament, paints a picture of victory for any believer in Christ. It portrays Jesus as having obtained victory and giving it over to his body the church. It is now our responsibility to discover what the scriptures tell us we have.

> **Jesus obtained eternal redemption for us. Falling into sin does not nullify our salvation in**

Whenever you read a scripture that seems to tell you to fight Satan, ask God to help you understand what it is really saying. This is important, because the Bible never contradicts itself. So, looking at verse 11, we understand that what we need to take a stand against, is the scheme or wiles of the forces of darkness.

Another way I used to see spiritual warfare was something like when Jacob wrestled with an angel of God all night. That also left me with the belief that sometimes you must force God to bless you, although he doesn't want to.

However, schemes/wiles are tricks meant to fool, entrap or entice. It follows that our fight is against believing the lies that the evil one tells us and which are meant to incapacitate us. To illustrate this better, I will use this analogy.

If you know that there are terrorists operating in the town you live in, and one day your spouse runs into the house, screaming that your neighborhood is about to come under attack, you will believe because you trust him. You probably will not try to venture out of the house after that. This is in spite of the fact that it is all a lie. In this situation, you are not held captive by terrorists, but by a lie. The lie will keep you in bondage until you find out the truth.

This is the same situation with Satan. Although he was defeated on the cross, children of God have not fully understood the completed work of Jesus on the cross, so he lies to them, and they are held captive. This is why Jesus said, "Then you shall know the truth and the truth shall make you free" John 8:32.

Another interesting scripture to buttress this point is found in **Hosea 4:6**

> "My people are destroyed for lack of knowledge. Because you have rejected knowledge, I also will reject you from being priest."

Also consider what **2 Corinthians 10:3-4** says;

> "For though we walk in the flesh, we do not war after the flesh: For the weapons of our warfare are not carnal, but mighty through God to the pulling down of strongholds.

> *We demolish arguments and every pretension that sets itself up against the knowledge of God, and we take captive every thought to make it obedient to Christ."*

This makes it clear that we are fighting the arguments and deceptions that spiritual forces of evil have used to hold us captive. Strongholds are fortresses built to keep people from escaping. In our own modern terminology, they are maximum security prisons in which people are held captive. Unfortunately, these are not physical walls holding people in, but mental walls built with lies that are carefully crafted by the father of all lies - Satan.

We are instructed to take captive every thought and make it obedient to Christ.

Isn't it interesting, that one of the most common beliefs of man, is that we cannot control our thoughts. This mindset is instilled in us from childhood. Early in life, our belief system and thought patterns are strategically targeted and shaped by Satan. Our unregenerate spirit causes us to think negatively, because it is void of the nature of God.

As a teacher, I have worked with many children who are highly talented, but are redundant because they are growing up believing they are dumb and have no value. You hear children calling each other retarded and dumb. I have had the joy of helping many change how they see themselves, and start pressing toward achieving something worthwhile with their lives.

As long as we believe this lie, we will never take responsibility for our thoughts and subsequently, our actions. Until you take charge of your thoughts, you will never experience freedom. This mindset is put in us very early in life, from childhood. Satan starts very early to shape our thought patterns. Our unregenerate spirit causes us to think negatively. As a teacher who works with children, as I stated earlier, I have seen highly intelligent kids waste their potential because they believe they are dumb and no good. After working with several and helping them paint a different mental picture, they are able to make tremendous gains academically.

What destroys and keeps us in bondage is our lack of knowledge of the truth of the word of God. Knowledge involves the use of your mind. The enemy is out to control our thought life. Taking a closer look at the armor of God, you see that it is not a physical thing; but all aspects of it have to do with things that influence our thinking. They are as follows:

- Belt of truth buckled around your waist
- Breastplate of righteousness

- Readiness from the gospel of peace
- Shield of faith
- Helmet of salvation
- Sword of the Spirit which is the Word of God

An interesting instruction is given to us in Ephesians 6:13, which is that we should put on the whole armor of God. It doesn't say some, but the whole armor of God. Paul does not instruct us to pray that God will put it on us. We are the ones that will do the putting on. This implies a conscious exercise of our will, and carrying out an action. He states clearly, that when we do so, we will be able to stand against ALL the wiles/deceptions of the evil one. This is profound! Below are the various components of the armor of God and what they mean to us.

Belt of Truth

From John 8:32 we understand that it is the knowledge of truth that sets us free. What do we need to be free from? We need to be free from lies which keep us in bondage. For the Roman soldier, the belt was what held his outfit in place. He hung his sword from the belt. The belt held his garments together so that his movement would not be hampered. Imagine a soldier at the peak of battle, trying to hold onto his loose garment to prevent his lower section from being exposed. He would most likely get killed in battle. Every Christian must be able to divide the word of truth accurately, or he will be put to shame by the enemy. What shame can be worse for a soldier than for his nakedness to be exposed?

On the other hand, the sword which is the word, hung on the belt. This implies that you must know how to use the word accurately; otherwise, it will become counterproductive. We are admonished to rightly divide the word of truth.

It is only the Holy Spirit that can reveal the truth of the word, because the letter kills, but the spirit gives life. The way we know we have the letter of the word is when we are not producing results. Religion is an imitation of a relationship with God. Paul clearly puts it this way in **2 Timothy 3:5:** *"Having a form of godliness, but denying the power thereof: from such turn away."*

I am bold to say that "Christianity" without power is not Christianity at all, but a bunch of religious rituals. It takes humility to tell yourself that something is wrong and it is at the belief level we must get this truth. The word of God has the ability to transform our lives. Jesus is truth, his life is an epitome of the true life we are meant to live, and our aspiration should be to live like he did. That is only possible through a knowledge of his word.

Why is righteousness a critical factor to winning spiritual warfare? It is because sin is what brought death and separation from the very abundant life of God. Once we are fully persuaded that sin has been dealt with, we will be bold to lay hold of our inheritance.

The Breastplate of Righteousness

For the Roman soldier, the breastplate was worn over the front of the body, to protect the torso. The section being protected included the vital organs of the body like the heart, liver, stomach and kidney. Any wound to this area could be deadly. The breastplate was often made of a solid piece of metal or smaller pieces of metal, fitted together like scales. This prevented weapons from reaching the body of the soldier. The knowledge that we have become the righteousness of God in Christ Jesus is crucial to the way we approach our fight against the kingdom of darkness.

The enemy uses sin-consciousness to keep us from coming against him. He is quick to remind us of our failures and sins. Once we feel condemned, we are unable to hold our ground against him. Praise be to God that we don't come against him in our own righteousness but by the blood of Jesus Christ. There is nothing we can ever do that is good enough to qualify us for answered prayer. We cannot grow in righteousness because it is not by our righteousness that God relates with us.

2 Corinthians 5:21

"For he hath made him to be sin for us. Who knew no sin; that we might be made the righteousness of God in him."

Romans 5:17

"...much more they which receive abundance of grace and of the gift of righteousness shall reign in life by one, Jesus Christ."

These scriptures are profound. Except you receive the free gift of righteousness and the abundant grace of God, you cannot reign over your circumstances in life. Grace simply put, is unmerited favor which provides us with free righteousness.

Righteousness can be defined as having a right standing with God. For better understanding, consider what it means to have a good standing with a bank. It implies that you do not default on your obligations, and this makes the bank willing to do business with you. Jesus gave us a good standing with God because he wiped out our debt, such that we owe nothing anymore. Hallelujah! The consciousness of such an amazing truth protects our vital organs and keeps us alive in spiritual warfare. Furthermore, without an understanding of the truth that we are righteous, we cannot walk in authority and exercise dominion over the powers of darkness. When Paul rebuked the Galatian church, he said in **Galatians 3:5-6:**

> *"So again I ask, does God give you his Spirit and work miracles among you by the works of the law, or by your believing what you heard? So also Abraham believed God, and it was credited to him as righteousness. Understand, then, that those who have faith are children of Abraham."*

We were made righteous by our faith in Jesus' finished work. It is also by faith that we receive the good things promised us in the word. It is only those who exercise faith that have access to the power of God. A sin-conscious believer cannot fight the enemy. He will lose, because the accuser of the brethren will continue to remind him of his failures, and this paralyzes him. In fact, if you rely on your works you bring yourself under a curse.

Galatians 3:10-13

> [10] *For all who rely on the works of the law are under a curse, as it is written: "Cursed is everyone who does not continue to do everything written in the Book of the Law."[e]* [11] *Clearly no one who relies on the law is justified before God, because "the righteous will live by faith."[f]* [12] *The law is not based on faith; on the contrary, it says, "The person who does these things will live by them."[g]* [13] *Christ redeemed us from the curse of the law*

> *by becoming a curse for us, for it is written: "Cursed is everyone who is hung on a pole."[h]*

I want to point out that non-Jews were never under the Laws of Moses. The Laws of Moses were put in place through the covenant God made on Mount Sinai with the Jews. So, in case you are reading this book and you are not a Jew, why are you trying to gain righteousness through a covenant you were never part of?

Finally, settle one thing in your heart, you can never meet God's standard for righteousness by your own efforts; regardless of how hard you try. It is impossible. In fact, the laws were meant to show us that we are wretched without a Saviour. So, quit trying, and receive the free gift of righteousness.

Readiness from the Gospel of Peace

Jesus is the Prince of peace, this is evidenced by what was announced at his birth by the angels.

Luke 2:14

> *Glory to God in the highest, and on earth peace, goodwill toward men.*

Isaiah 9:6

> *"....The everlasting Father, The Prince of Peace."*

Except we have experienced peace with God, how can we be ready to push back the forces of darkness. If your mindset is that God is fighting you, and against you because of something you did wrong, you will never have the boldness to stand your ground against the onslaught of the devil. The word "gospel" means good news. Putting it all together, it tells us there is a readiness that comes with the good news of peace, which is why Jesus came. Knowing and having peace of mind in every area of our lives is one of the reasons why Jesus came. Peace does not mean the absence of challenges, but the knowledge of the truth that God is with you in every situation. Consider Jesus who was in the middle of a deadly storm, yet he was fast asleep while his disciples fretted. Think about whenever you are worried about a problem in your life. It consumes you so much that you are unable to focus on other issues in your life. Worry and lack of peace will affect your relationships, jobs and health.

Absence of peace is the reason many will never fulfil their destinies. This is because their thoughts are held captive by worry. All their energy is directed towards resolving the same issues. Unfortunately, we forget that problems are part of life and Jesus gave us his peace which is superior to what the world can ever give us. Worry is indeed a grievous sin against

God. Many Christians say they are human and that is why they worry. Yet, they do not realize that the children of Israel perished in the wilderness because they were too worried to trust God with their needs.

Decide to enter into a place of peace which is a fruit of the Holy Ghost, given to us by Jesus. This will give you confidence to take on the devil. We will speak the word of God with confidence, and not be afraid that God will not hear us.

John 14:27

> *Peace I leave with you; my peace I give you. I do not give to you as the world gives. Do not let your hearts be troubled and do not be afraid.*

With your feet wearing the gospel of peace, you will run into battle knowing that God will never leave nor forsake you, and victory is sure.

Shield of Faith

The soldier uses the shield to protect himself from all the fiery darts of the enemy. Fiery darts as the name implies are arrows that are on fire, which are shot at us by the devil. These are words which if we allow to get to us, will set our lives on fire. Remember what we are fighting against are not the demons, but their strategic lies which are used to attack what we know. Our shield of faith is what protects us, because we have come to believe what the word says, and are able to discern truth from lies.

Any Christian who will be strong in faith will have to know the word. **Our fight is a fight of faith.**
1 Timothy 6:12
> *Fight the good fight of faith. Take hold of the eternal life to which you were called when you made your good confession in the presence of many witnesses.*

We fight to stand our ground in faith until our victory manifests. The Bible defines faith as "the substance of things hoped for, the evidence of things not seen". I have come to understand this as meaning that the word of God is our substance. It is the visible word of God which we read that gives us substance or something to hold onto, and which assures us that his promise will come to pass. Without seeing a promise in the word of God, there is no basis for believing that we will receive anything from God.

Secondly, Abraham was counted righteous because he had faith in God. Righteousness is what gives us confidence to approach God in prayer. The unrighteous do not have access into God's presence.

Hebrews 10:22

> *Let us draw near to God with a sincere heart and with the full assurance that faith brings, having our hearts*

sprinkled to cleanse us from a guilty conscience and having our bodies washed with pure water. Let us hold fast the confession of our hope without wavering for he that promised is faithful.

There is a boldness that comes with faith which is needed to stand your ground no matter the lies that are shot at you. Consider that prior to this scripture, the chapter was talking about the forgiveness of sin and the truth that God does not remember our sins any more. It encourages us to hold unswervingly to our faith. What faith is this? Saving faith! This faith is not produced by ourselves, but is a gift from God (Ephesians 2:8-9).

This is the faith that gives us confidence to get hold of everything that comes with salvation. We don't need any other faith to obtain anything from God. Yet for many Christians, when it comes to our needs being met, we feel we need to get more faith. It is only this faith that gives us confidence to draw near to God, and take authority over all the wiles of the enemy. What faith can be greater than the one that translated us from the kingdom of darkness into that of God's marvelous light?

Helmet of Salvation

The Roman soldier wore a metal helmet to protect his head. An unprotected head could spell death in battle. The head is where the brain which controls the thinking process is. A simple stone slung by David, hit Goliath's unprotected forehead and killed him instantly (1 Samuel 17:40-49). Think about this, Goliath was a giant but was killed by a teenager. This shows that we must protect our minds with the knowledge and confidence that we are saved. We should never at any time doubt our salvation, because if you do, you become unsure of your place in Christ. Jesus obtained eternal redemption for us. Falling into sin does not nullify our salvation in Christ.

Hebrews 9:12

> *He entered once for all into the holy place, not by means of the blood of goats and calves but by means of his own blood, thus securing an eternal redemption.*

Jesus paid for all our sins, past, present and future once and for all. Think about it, was any of us alive when he shed his blood on Calvary? While on Calvary, he was paying for our future sins, because we weren't even born. Let us be confident in the knowledge that our salvation is secure and cannot be taken away from us. We can choose to throw it away, or trample it underfoot by rejecting Jesus. This happens when we denounce him with our lips, and refuse to believe in him as our Lord and Saviour. God does not disown us when we sin against him.

When we deny and reject what he has done for us through our verbal confession, he has no choice but to let us go. This truth is supported by the following scriptures:

2 Timothy 2:13

> [11] This is a faithful saying: For if we died with Him. We shall also live with Him. [12] If we endure, We shall also reign with Him. If we deny Him, He also will deny us. [13] If we are faithless, He remains faithful; He cannot deny Himself.

Hebrews 13:5

> [5] Keep your lives free from the love of money and be content with what you have, because God has said, "Never will I leave you; never will I forsake you."

We get born again by believing and receiving Jesus into our heart. When we believed, we confessed him as Lord. It was not by any act of righteousness that we got saved. The implication is that it is only by doing the opposite that we forfeit our inheritance in the kingdom of God.

Romans 10:10

> ¹⁰ *For it is with your heart that you believe and are justified, and it is with your mouth that you profess your faith and are saved.*

Ephesians 2:8-9

> ⁸ *For it is by grace you have been saved, through faith— and this is not from yourselves, it is the gift of God—* ⁹ *not by works, so that no one can boast.*

Bear in mind that when the Bible talks about being saved, it isn't just referring to going to heaven. When Jesus died on the cross, he delivered us from everything that came upon us as a result of the fall of man in the Garden of Eden. When man fell, he lost the ability to live in dominion. Jesus met the requirements of God's justice. As I mentioned earlier in this book, sickness, poverty, pain, suffering and fear became man's portion. Jesus' last words on the cross were, "It is finished". Just as we did nothing but believe to obtain salvation from sin, we also do not have to do more than that to reign in life.

It is therefore extremely important to be fully persuaded mentally about what your salvation truly is when you are a soldier of Christ. When we have an iota of doubt or confusion, our enemy will latch on it to convince us that we don't qualify for what we are trusting God for.

Salvation can be understood by considering earthly relationships. Good parents do not disown and disinherit their children when they commit a crime. Neither do children cease to be part of a family because of bad behavior. You inherit a family name through birth and not because of your behavior. To lose a family name, either the child has to initiate the process or the government may take a child away from his parents. Either way, it involves a lot of paperwork and the judicial system to drop a family name. In the same way, it takes a long process to bring a onetime believer to a point of losing salvation and it will have to be by the choice of the individual, not God's. The believer renounces God, and when that happens, God will have no choice but to do the same.

Sword of the Spirit

The sword of the spirit is the word of God. The word of God is Jesus.

John 1:1

In the beginning was the Word and the Word was with God and the Word was God.

The sword of the Spirit which we use against our enemy is Jesus. If we speak the word, we send forth Jesus whom Satan and his cohorts can never stand up against. He is not dead, but alive forevermore. He never lost a battle, and that is why we should never lose one. When we grasp the truth that all scripture is a revelation of Jesus Christ, and speak it, the enemy is bound to turn around and flee.

Hebrews 4:12

> *For the word of God is alive and active. Sharper than any double-edged sword, it penetrates even to dividing soul and spirit, joints and marrow; it judges the thoughts and attitudes of the heart.*

The soldier in Bible times used the sword to kill or hurt his enemy. This is similar to what we use guns for today. As a double edged sword, the word will cut in both directions. Effective use of the word of God helps us discern what is from the flesh and what is from the spirit. No Christian can succeed by living in the flesh. Our thoughts can easily deceive us, but by lifting the word against it, we are able to judge what is coming from the Spirit or the flesh. Living in the realm of the flesh, we come under the enemy's control. The word is God's standard for living.

It is only the word of God that the devil responds to, not our opinions. We use it to destroy every lie, argument and deception of the devil which is indeed what we are up against.

Psalm 138:2

> I will worship toward Your holy temple, And praise Your name For Your lovingkindness and Your truth; For You have magnified Your word above all Your name.

Isaiah 55:11

> So shall My word be that goes forth from My mouth;

It shall not return to Me void, But it shall accomplish what I please, And it shall prosper in the thing for which I sent it.

These verses tell us how powerful the word of God is. The word of God is powerful and is intended to accomplish what it is sent to do. God created the world by faith and it was through his spoken word. We are made in the image of God, and should create our lives by speaking the word of God.

Unfortunately, many find it easier to speak human opinions and feelings than the word. We get results by the continuous use of the word on our situation.

I remember a day when I was attacked by symptoms of the flu. My head was pounding, I also had high fever and body aches. In spite of what I was feeling, I stood on the word of God, and claimed my healing. The symptoms didn't seem to be abating and I also refused to stop speaking the word. By the end of the day, my whole body was very weak. I went to bed speaking the word, and when I woke up the next day, all symptoms were gone and my strength restored. Flu infections are supposed to last for one to two weeks but with my standing on the word and resisting the enemy, I was healed. Praise God.

Another proof that standing on the word will bring great results, was in my finances. I remember the time we needed to prepare to pay college fees for my two kids. Two years prior, I decided that I would start to trust God to provide for me, and not use credit cards to meet my financial needs. I also pledged not to ask anybody for money. At this point, it was less than two weeks to the deadline for payments, and I still didn't have the money. In addition to this, my children were owing money from the previous semester and couldn't register for classes for the winter semester. This was going to cost me some thousands of Dollars. They kept reminding me that they needed to pay their old balance. All I could tell them was that my God was going to supply all my needs according to his riches in glory. They definitely were not excited about my attitude.

An interesting thing happened. My daughter called to tell me she had been on the phone with her school for over an hour and they told her the school owed her some thousands of dollars from the previous semester. They also told her she didn't have to pay a dime for the new semester because her scholarship covered it. We rejoiced over the miracle, although we didn't understand how that could be. However, my son still needed to pay his balance. The enemy kept telling me that there was no way out of this situation, because I had no way of raising the necessary funds. The Sunday before the deadline, I asked God to lead me in my giving. I pledged a certain amount in church as my first fruits. I continued to tell God I trusted him to provide, regardless of what my circumstances looked like.

The following morning, I was awakened by a phone call from Nigeria. My sister in law, whom I hadn't told what was going on called, requesting for my bank account details. She told me my brother wanted to send me some money. The money I received was enough to pay my son's debt and also meet other needs. On making the payment, my son was told he had a credit balance which had been applied to his new semester fees. As a result, I didn't need to pay any fees that semester. Till date, I still don't understand how the school handled his fees, and I honestly don't want to figure it out.

One thing we can observe from Matthew 4:1-11, is

that Jesus was tempted through his thoughts. The devil didn't appear physically to Jesus, this is the same way he comes to us.

The enemy is no match for the word of God when it is spoken in faith. The enemy is not affected by our reasoning or pleading with him. When he came against Jesus in the wilderness, he tried to plant doubt in Jesus' mind about his sonship. Jesus didn't try to convince Satan that he was the Son of God. For each temptation, Jesus responded with the word, "It is written..." Notice also that even the devil quoted the scriptures to Jesus, but it was tweaked up to his advantage. What then was the catch on the devil's side? He wanted Jesus to use the scriptures to achieve his personal agenda, but this is not the purpose of the word of God. God expects us to use his word to glorify him not ourselves. Jesus knew that God's will was that he gets the kingdom back by going to the cross, not through bowing to the devil.

Having analyzed all the components of the armor of God, it is crucial to note that absolutely no provision was made to protect the back side of the soldier. The implication is that God expects us to suit up, hold our ground and advance. God does not permit us to look back or turn back while in battle. Luke 17:32 Remember Lot's wife.

Hebrews 10:38 (NIV)

> "But my righteous[a] one will live by faith. And I take no pleasure in the one who shrinks back."

Shrinking or drawing away from battle in unbelief, is evidence that we have lost faith; and this exposes us to being a prime target for destruction by our adversary.

Lot's wife was turned into a pillar of salt because she looked back at what she had left behind. In the same way, God has asked us to continue moving forward in our walk with him and taking new territories. The further we go, the closer we are to obtaining the price to which we are called. Every step taken forward, is a step indicating that we have left another thing we don't need for our goal behind. Why then should we retreat out of fear?

We can also learn from the children of Israel who left the land of Egypt, but ended up dying in the desert without ever taking possession of the Promised Land. Their problem was unbelief, and the fact that they were always looking and going back in their hearts to Egypt. They constantly thought about it, and that was why they spoke about it. For us to win the fight of faith, we need to settle in our hearts that it is forward ever, backward never. It is more honorable to die fighting than to die retreating. The good news is that when we are in faith, victory is assured.

Chapter 2

Pray

Ephesians 6:18

> *¹⁸ And pray in the Spirit on all occasions with all kinds of prayers and requests. With this in mind, be alert and always keep on praying for all the Lord's people.*

Prayer has been largely misunderstood by mankind. As we all know, in every religion, people pray. The religious art of prayer is something that makes man feel better when done. As Christians we need to understand what prayer really should be. It is a time of communication with God. The first prayer took place in Genesis 3, after man fell into sin, and God came looking for them. Isn't it interesting that although man had sinned, God still spoke to them, and even told them what their future was going to be. From this place, we see that prayer is a two-way conversation with God. It does not have to involve asking God for anything at all. Before the fall, man communed with God but didn't ask him for anything because they already had all they needed.

From this we can deduce that the primary reason for prayer is not to ask but to fellowship. In fellowship, you get to know the heart and nature of a person. Fellowship reveals a personality to you, and you know people from listening to them. When you do most of the talking, you reveal yourself to a person, not the other way.

The good thing about fellowshipping with God,

and getting to know him, is that you also get to know who you are. This is because, you are made in God's image and have his nature. If we truly grasp our identity as royalty, it becomes clear to us that royalty commands authority. Princes do not beg any man, rather they live by making decrees. This brings us back to why authority is our covenant right because we have been drafted into the family of God.

Another thing we need to remember is that prayer must line up with the word of God.

In many Christian circles, prayer is seen as a tool to make God do something. We hear terms like "bombarding heaven" and "bringing heaven down". This gives the impression that God is reluctant to do something, and if we pray hard and long enough, we will get him to help us.

Nothing is further from the truth than this. God is our father, and desires to supply all we need according to his riches in glory. When we have a vibrant fellowship with God, his will becomes ours, and we are able to call his will into existence on earth. The Spirit of God knows what his mind is, and that same spirit dwells in us, because he is our seal for the day of redemption.

God does not permit us to look back or turn back while in battle.

In Ephesians 6:18, we are admonished to pray in the Spirit. The term praying in the Spirit has been interpreted to mean different things by many people. However, this is what the Bible says in **1 Corinthians 14:13-15:**

> [13] *"For this reason, the one who speaks in a tongue should pray that they may interpret what they say.* [14] *For if I pray in a tongue, my spirit prays, but my mind is unfruitful.* [15]

> *So what shall I do? I will pray with my spirit, but I will also pray with my understanding; I will sing with my spirit, but I will also sing with my understanding."*

These scriptures clearly define what it means to pray in the Holy Ghost. When we pray in the Spirit, it is our spirit which is born of God that prays for us. It prays a perfect, unbiased prayer to God. The most dynamic aspect of this exercise is the fact that the enemy does not understand what is being said. This makes it impossible for him to interfere with what we are trying to get. When we pray in our understanding, we approach the situation on hand with our human understanding. We judge it based on our five senses unlike when the spirit prays through us.

In addition to this, the Bible tells us that praying in the Holy Ghost is a means by which we edify ourselves. We recharge our spiritual battery. We all know that you cannot start a car if the battery is weak. The newest of cars will not start if the battery is not charged. We can't stand up against the evil one or be effective when we are not charged up. The gift of praying in the Spirit is the only spiritual gift which is said to edify the believer who does it. The rest of the gifts like prophecy are for the benefit of the people being ministered to.

Like the car used as an example, without being charged up, even the most technologically advanced car is of no use to the driver. This means that when we are not charged up through praying in tongues, we will not have the strength to stand against the devil or exercise the other spiritual gifts provided for building up the body of Christ. I am convinced that this is why the issue of praying in tongues has been under continuous attack by the forces of darkness. From telling Christians that the gift died with the apostles, to whispering to them that they are making no sense when speaking in tongues, many get cold feet about the concept. On the other hand, many who actually believe and receive the gift of praying in the Spirit, are ignorant of the power in this spiritual exercise. It is time to use this as a weapon to cause confusion in the kingdom of darkness.

A while ago, I had an experience that showed how effective praying in tongues can be. I was on the train going home from work when I felt a heaviness on my heart. I normally read my Bible on the train, but that evening, I felt a strong impression to pray in the Spirit. I prayed in tongues for a while and heard in my heart that I was actually interceding for a colleague whose son had kidney failure. The Holy Spirit told me to ask her how he was doing the next day.

Getting to work the next day, I completely forgot about it. However, I overheard her telling another colleague that around the same time, her son's fiancée who was with him in another state at the hospital had called and texted her, but she for some reason didn't receive them. Her son was undergoing dialysis and went into shock and became unconscious. Fortunately, God brought him out of it. Immediately, I remembered how the Holy Spirit had led me to intercede for him at that time and I told her. My colleague confessed she would have freaked out had she received the text or call. God in his mercy prevented her from receiving the message but led me to intervene through praying in tongues. This averted a tragedy.

Praise as a weapon of Warfare

Recall that Lucifer's greatest desire was to make himself greater and higher than God. He was the archangel in charge of worship in heaven and by being higher than God, all the angels would have worshipped him if he had succeeded. Glory to God, his plans failed. However, he still seeks people to worship him. Think about how much you hated to be around, as an unbeliever, when someone you envied was being praised. The implication is that we can actually send the devil running when we get into high praise. When we praise God, we are telling him how good he is, and appreciating his nature. Praise is always in line with the word of God which releases power. I believe that one of the most powerful scriptures in the Bible that points out the importance of praise in spiritual warfare is found in **Psalm 149:6-9.**

> *May the praise of God be in their mouths and a double-edged sword in their hands, [7] to inflict vengeance on the nations and punishment on the peoples, [8] to bind their kings with fetters, their nobles with shackles of iron, [9] to carry out the sentence written against them—this is the glory of all his faithful people.*

In verse 6 we see that praise goes hand in hand with the word of God. These two things are weapons of war with which we are able to inflict injuries on the enemy and stop him in his tracks. The word of God is the only weapon we've been given which inflicts casualties on the forces of darkness. Ephesians 6:17 calls the word of God the sword of the spirit, it is used to extinguish all the fiery darts of the evil one.

A familiar example in scripture is the story of Paul

and Silas in Acts 16:23-27, they were flogged severely with rods and imprisoned because of their faith in Christ. Although they were in great pain and distress, they chose to give God praise audibly. They were so loud that the other prisoners heard them. While this was going on, suddenly God sent an earthquake which resulted in the chains falling off their hands and feet. They were immediately set free. Glory to God, there is power in praise and we need to use it to execute judgement on the forces of darkness.

> **Many who actually believe and receive the gift of praying in the Spirit, are ignorant of the power in this spiritual exercise.**

Throughout the Bible, praise and worship has been shown to put man in a position of dominance over the forces of darkness. This is because God inhabits the praises of his people. Praise brings the glory of God down to where you are. This routs the kingdom of darkness, and brings positive changes to situations.

Another reason why praise is an instrument with which we exercise authority over the kingdom of darkness is because it drives away fear from us. When we don't do it as a show or religiously, it stirs up boldness in us, and fear automatically runs away. When King Jehoshaphat was faced with an impossible situation, the word of the Lord came to him saying "Fear not". This story is found in 2 Chronicles 20:1-27, and it illustrates the power in praise and worship. Praise causes you to take the focus off your humanity and fix your eyes on God and his abilities as mentioned in verse 12. Many times, we claim to be praising God in our minds. It is good to praise God in your heart, but let it flow out from within you audibly, so that the devil and his cohorts can hear you. Remember, the devil cannot read your mind.

The third reason to praise God is because when we praise God, we speak the truth of God because it talks of the nature of God: his goodness and greatness. Our words of praise is our strength, because we are speaking God into our battles. On the flip side, when we praise our problems through worry and speaking words of unbelief, we lift up the enemy and give him an upper hand.

Chapter 3

The Purpose of Trials and Troubles

For a long time, I didn't understand why trouble comes to believers. I wondered; if Satan is defeated, why do we still have to "fight" him? I remember when I had two consecutive years of roller coaster trials and troubles. Several times, I felt that things couldn't get more challenging, but they did, and I wondered how much more I would have to face. However, the Holy Spirit started to show me why we get tried. First of all, there's a God perspective and a Satan perspective. The story is told of Jesus and his disciples being confronted with a storm.

The Purpose of Trials and Troubles

Matthew 8:23-27

> *²³ Then he got into the boat and his disciples followed him. ²⁴ Suddenly a furious storm came up on the lake, so that the waves swept over the boat. But Jesus was sleeping. ²⁵ The disciples went and woke him, saying, "Lord, save us! We're going to drown!"*
>
> *²⁶ He replied, "You of little faith, why are you so afraid?" Then he got up and rebuked the winds and the waves, and it was completely calm. ²⁷ The men were amazed and asked, "What kind of man is this? Even the winds and the waves obey him!"*

This story is particularly interesting, because it is a good illustration of what we face as children of God. Earlier on that day, Jesus had spent time teaching and doing miracles. After everything, he asked his disciples to get into a boat with him and go to the other side of the lake. Shortly after the journey started, he fell asleep and a big storm hit, threatening to drown them.

The question is, was Jesus not aware that a storm was on the way? Why then did he take them on a perilous journey? Does it mean that God wants to see us suffer or get into dangerous situations? Did God send them the storm? Many people claim that God sends trouble to us.

The truth is that, God didn't send the storm but he knew it was going to come. Satan sent the storm in his continued effort to destroy the people of God. Satan, being a liar, believes he is capable of destroying God's purpose for our lives. Although Jesus knew a storm was coming, it didn't make him change his plans of going to the other side of the lake. Jesus knew who he was, and was aware that nothing could take his life or harm him. Although the disciples had seen and heard the word of God at work, they didn't fully grasp the power in the word available to them. This was why they became afraid when they saw the winds and the waves. Their fear was motivated by their senses: what they saw and heard, rather than the spoken word from Jesus.

Fortunately, they ran to Jesus for help although they could have used the word of God to take care of the situation. Jesus rebuked the wind and it calmed down. One of the most important things I learned from this is that Jesus could have slept through the storm and still arrived at the other side of the lake. It is obvious to me that he rebuked the storm for the sake of his disciples. Left to Jesus, he would have been riding the storm. To prove this, I would like to make reference to the story in Matthew 14:22-31.

Matthew 14: 22,

> "*Immediately Jesus made the disciples get into the boat and go on ahead of him to the other side, while he dismissed the crowd.* ^{23} *After he had dismissed them, he went up on a mountainside*

by himself to pray. Later that night, he was there alone, ²⁴ and the boat was already a considerable distance from land, buffeted by the waves because the wind was against it. ²⁵ Shortly before dawn Jesus went out to them, walking on the lake. ²⁶ When the disciples saw him walking on the lake, they were terrified. "It's a ghost," they said, and cried out in fear. ²⁷ But Jesus immediately said to them: "Take courage! It is I. Don't be afraid." ²⁸ "Lord, if it's you," Peter replied, "tell me to come to you on the water." ²⁹ "Come," he said. Then Peter got down out of the boat, walked on the water and came toward Jesus. ³⁰ But when he saw the wind, he was afraid and, beginning to sink, cried out, "Lord, save me!" ³¹ Immediately Jesus reached out his hand and caught him. "You of little faith," he said, "why did you doubt?"

Notice that in verse 25 Jesus came walking on the lake, while they were buffeted by the waves, it is

The Purpose of Trials and Troubles

obvious the storm was irrelevant to Jesus getting across the lake. Once Jesus climbed into their boat, the wind died down, even without him rebuking it. In this instance, Jesus was fully aware of an impending storm, yet he told them to get into the boat and travel to the other side.

As believers, we must understand that storms of life will come from the enemy, for the purpose of hurting us. God may also send us into a stormy situation, not because he wants it to harm us, but for us to ride the storm and take control of it. When we exercise victory over the storms of life, people around us will exclaim, "What kind of man is this? Even the winds and the waves obey him!" This is the authority we have been given, and are expected to display as sons of the Most High God. There is no other way the world will see the difference if we don't change our mindset about the troubles of life. God is our father and a great one at that. He knows what we can handle, and will not lead us into circumstances beyond us. We are made in his image, and endowed with supernatural potentials which must be demonstrated when trouble comes our way.

Also realize that in both stories, Jesus was not sympathetic toward them when they cried in unbelief and fear. It is disappointing to God when his children shrink back in the face of trouble, and refuse to stand their ground against the evil one. Jesus actually rebuked them. Having been made kings and priests of the Most

> **It is one thing to say you believe that God's word is powerful but another to believe that when you speak it, it is also effective.**

The Purpose of Trials and Troubles

High God, there is no room for crying and self-pity, because we are fully equipped to deal with the troubles of this life. God would be wicked and unjust to lead us into precarious situations that are beyond our abilities. Everyday we wake up, we should remind ourselves of whose and who we are.

For us to thrive in the midst of life's troubles, we must learn to keep our eyes focused fully on the word of God which is relevant to our situation. Constant focus on the physical evidence will render our faith unproductive. The physical will normally contradict the word. The physical is controlled by our adversary, and he uses it to convince us that the word is not working and true. To come out victorious, our confession must be, "If God said it, I believe it, and that settles it".

Secondly, you must believe that the word of God you speak is as powerful as the one God speaks. You must be fully convinced that you are the oracle of the Most High God. It is one thing to say you believe that God's word is powerful, but another to believe that when you speak it, it is also effective. The problem is that we judge the power in our words based on our behavior. When we live right, we see ourselves as powerful but if we sin, we feel powerless. Remember it is all about Jesus and his finished work.

Thirdly, what I would like to point out is what the disciples did in Luke 8:23-25. This story is the same as that of Matthew 8:23-31, which I wrote about earlier. However, Luke gave a detail missing in Matthew's account. Luke wrote that the disciples were bailing water out from the boat. This is synonymous with our self-effort in the midst of life's challenges. Most of us will try and work our way out

The Purpose of Trials and Troubles

of trouble because we see issues as merely physical. The problem was that the storm was a spiritual attack caused by forces of darkness. Had it been in our generation, the meteorologists would have explained why there was a storm. I am not saying that meteorologists are wrong in giving reasons for storms and natural disasters. However, we must understand that in the Garden of Eden, there were no tornadoes, hurricanes and earthquakes. This was because all creation existed in a perfect state until sin entered, and death and destruction immediately came into play.

From this, we can see that when things get bad, there are negative forces at work. It then follows that by bailing out water, the disciples were not going to be able to save themselves. Another thing is that they were unable to move forward in the direction they were headed while bailing out water.

However, when they brought Jesus into the situation, he did a simple thing, he rebuked the storm. He spoke loud and clear and immediately the storm ceased. Always remember that we live in a physical world which is controlled by the spiritual. Learn to speak the word with authority and save yourself some energy, time and effort.

Another reason why we have trials and temptations is because we live in a fallen world.

John 9:1-4

> *As he went along, he saw a man blind from birth. [2] His disciples asked him, "Rabbi, who sinned, this man or his parents, that he was born blind?" [3] "Neither this man nor his parents sinned," said Jesus, "but this happened so that the works of God might be displayed in him. [4] As long as it is day, we must do the works of him who sent me. Night is coming, when no one can work. [5] While I am in the world, I am the light of the world."*

John 10:10

> *The thief comes only to steal and kill and destroy; I have come that they may have life, and have it to the full.*

Putting these scriptures together, we can deduce that even without sinning, trouble can come to the best of us. This is why you hear of children born with cancer and other life-threatening illnesses. The god of this world, Satan is doing his work of killing, stealing and destroying. Death is naturally at work in our mortal bodies, but we can stop it with the authority provided by the cross.

Note that John 9 isn't implying that God did it or allowed it to happen. God had no hand in it, because Jesus came to give life not death. Satan is the one that steals and kills, which is why the man was blind. Jesus came to destroy the works of the evil one. Notice what Jesus did immediately he made the statement in verse 4, and what he did as you read down to verse 8. From this particular story, it is clear what our responsibility is when we see any work of Satan. We are expected to change it from evil to good. That is the work which we all have been called to do. God expects us to be like Jesus.

Jesus had rivers of living water flowing through him and when we have the Holy Spirit in us, so do we.

John 7

> *37 In the last day, that great day of the feast, Jesus stood and cried, saying, If any man thirst, let him come unto me, and drink. 38 He that believeth on me, as the scripture hath said, out of his belly shall flow rivers of living water. 39 (But this spake he of the Spirit, which they that believe on him should receive: for the Holy Ghost was not yet given; because that Jesus was not yet glorified.)*

In John 4, Jesus was speaking to the Samaritan woman and told her that if she believed in him, she would have a well of living water welling up to

The Purpose of Trials and Troubles

eternal life. However, in John 7, we hear Jesus taking it up a notch. He talked about rivers of living water, flowing out of your belly/heart up to eternal life. Jesus clearly states that this was referring to the Holy Spirit whom was to come after he was glorified. The Holy Spirit was given on the day of Pentecost. It follows that once you receive the baptism in the Holy Spirit, you become a source of rivers of living water. This isn't one river but rivers. Life refers to the God kind of life, prosperity, health, peace, joy, complete wholeness in every area of existence. You don't just have it for yourself, but make it available to a lot of people. The differences between a well or spring (John 4:14) and rivers (John 7:38) are numerous:

1. A well can dry up, but rivers don't easily get dry.

2. A well has limited reach. A river can bless several nations and people. Good examples are the River Nile and the Mississippi River.
3. Wells are used to meet basic domestic needs, while rivers can be used for irrigation, transportation, fishing, sporting and much more.

So, get a mental picture of what Jesus is saying happens when you receive the baptism of the Spirit. You become a person fully loaded to touch and change nations. This is our heritage as children of the Most High God. Let us recognize the rivers of living water that are flowing out of us.

Jesus had rivers of life flowing out of him. When he and his disciples needed tax money, he sent Peter to catch a fish, and in its mouth was the provision. When they had an outreach of over 5,000 people and they got hungry, he took five loaves and two

The Purpose of Trials and Troubles

fishes, and used it to feed everyone. At the end, 12 baskets of leftover were collected. When Lazarus fell ill and died, he raised him up from the dead. When he entered into several cities and villages, every manner of disease was healed. I could go on and on. Those were all rivers of living water flowing out of him. Hallelujah!! That was the kingdom at work through him.

The final reason I will mention in this chapter for trials and troubles can be found in **Deuteronomy 8:3:**

> [3] *And he humbled thee, and suffered thee to hunger, and fed thee with manna, which thou knewest not, neither did thy fathers know; that he might make thee know that man doth not live by bread only, but by every word that proceedeth out of the mouth of the Lord doth man live.*

When God took the children of Israel through the wilderness, he allowed them to hunger, not so that they could starve to death, but so they could learn to depend on his word for their daily provision. When they came out of Egypt, they had provision. They came out with some amount of food, but they eventually ran out of their own provision. They were brought to a place of impossibility, and needed God. It is funny to think that they forgot that without God, they couldn't have made it that far. So, trials come so that we can learn to depend on the word of God.

Yes, our lives ought to be completely anchored on the spoken word of God. Had Israel learned this lesson early in their journey, they would have made

> **We let the present challenges of life overshadow the testimonies from the past.**

The Purpose of Trials and Troubles

it into the Promised Land. Alas they didn't, and ended up perishing in the wilderness of "just enough". It is very sad to see that this is the story of many children of God.

We let the present challenges of life overshadow the testimonies from the past. We forget that the God who spoke is faithful and that the life he promised is an abundant one. A life of continuous, total victory. A life where we reign as kings on earth.

Chapter 4

According to Your Faith

Having grown up in churches where we were taught that getting blessed depends on God, it is no wonder that I constantly pleaded with God for blessings.

Honestly, most times I felt I didn't deserve anything from him because of my shortcomings. I am thankful that today I know better. It is important to understand that if a promise is going to be fulfilled, it is my responsibility to agree with the scripture and receive it by faith. I didn't need to attain a certain level of righteousness to receive from God. God is able to do exceedingly, abundantly, above all I can ever ask or think. He goes further to declare in Isaiah

1:19 If you are willing and obedient, you will eat the good things of the land.

If I ever enjoy the blessings of God, it will be because I decided to agree with this verse. It is always faith that brings to pass the promises of God. All the people that received healing from Jesus exercised their faith. In fact, the woman with the issue of blood for 12 years, received her healing without Jesus being involved. She used her faith to draw healing out of Jesus without his permission. She acted on Jesus' proclamation in Luke 4:18, of what his ministry on earth was all about. He proclaimed that he came to preach deliverance to the captives, so she took hold of her deliverance based on his words.

My simple definition of faith is stepping out on the word of God. When Peter stepped out of the boat to walk on water, he did it because Jesus spoke the word "Come." Peter stepped out on that one word and as long as he stood on it, he walked on water. However, once he took his focus off the word and started looking at the wind and the waves, he began to sink. We shouldn't blame or hold God responsible for the negative things we are faced with. Satan is the one that sends them our way. We need to take responsibility for changing it by joining hands with God through his word. God has designed our relationship with him in such a way that we have a part to play in our own destiny. Our exercise of faith is key.

All the faith we need already indwells us as children of God. This faith was deposited in our spirit by the indwelling Holy Spirit. He produces the fruit of faith in us and we bear it - showing it forth as a branch shows forth fruit. Exercising our faith when challenged by the enemy, strengthens it and causes us to experience victory. So today, exercise your faith muscles by using them.

Every one of us in the body of Christ carries the same level of authority. This statement will shock many Christians. This is because many of us depend on others to handle Satan for us. We feel some people are more powerful in the kingdom than others. This mindset shouldn't be. None of us can handle Satan in our own strength. It is Jesus who overcame him not any man. The difference amongst believers is in knowledge and your willingness to exercise spiritual authority with boldness and faith.

My heart breaks to see believers make idols of "Men of God". They see these popular ministers as

> **It is my responsibility to agree with the scripture and receive it by faith.**

demigods, without understanding that what these people have they have also. Peter made this clear in Acts 4 and returned all glory to God when he healed the crippled man.

> [12] *And when Peter saw it, he answered unto the people, Ye men of Israel, why marvel ye at this? or why look ye so earnestly on us, as though by our own power or holiness we had made this man to walk?* [16] *And his name through faith in his name hath made this man strong, whom ye see and know: yea, the faith which is by him hath given him this perfect soundness in the presence of you all.*

Anyone that develops their relationship with God is capable of experiencing the supernatural. It is a shame that some well-known preachers love attention and glory instead of encouraging believers to seek God for themselves.

Chapter 5

Learn from Israel

How does an 11-day journey take 40 years to be accomplished? This was what happened to the Israelites. What can we learn from the children of Israel whom Moses was chosen to lead into Canaan, the Promised Land? God handpicked them from all the nations of the earth to be his special people.

Deuteronomy 14:2

> "For thou art an holy people unto the LORD thy God, and the LORD hath chosen thee to be a peculiar people unto himself, above all the nations that are upon the earth."

Everything that happened to Israel is a type and shadow of what could happen to us, the church. We are spiritual Israel; the people of God called to be his set apart ones. As we have been learning, God has in store for us a Promised Land. We have been called to be a royal priesthood.

We will look closely at Israel's journey from Egypt to Canaan. Remember, not every child of God will experience this glorious life on earth.

1 Corinthians 10:1-11

> *For I do not want you to be ignorant of the fact, brothers and sisters, that our ancestors were all under the cloud and that they all passed through the sea. ² They were all baptized into Moses in the cloud and in the sea. ³ They all ate the same spiritual food ⁴ and drank the same spiritual drink; for they drank from the spiritual rock that accompanied them, and that rock was Christ. ⁵ Nevertheless, God was not pleased with most of them;*

Learn from Israel

their bodies were scattered in the wilderness. [6] Now these things occurred as examples to keep us from setting our hearts on evil things as they did. [7] Do not be idolaters, as some of them were; as it is written: The people sat down to eat and drink and got up to indulge in revelry. [a] [8] We should not commit sexual immorality, as some of them did—and in one day twenty-three thousand of them died. [9] We should not test Christ, [b] as some of them did—and were killed by snakes. [10] And do not grumble, as some of them did—and were killed by the destroying angel.

[11] These things happened to them as examples and were written down as warnings for us, on whom the culmination of the ages has come

Be aware that all the adults aged 20 years and above, didn't enter into the Promised Land except for Caleb and Joshua. Even Moses who led them was not allowed into the land of Canaan. This chapter states that they all ate the same food from heaven, drank from the same rock, and were under the same cloud (the Holy Spirit). Also, they all saw God judge the land of Egypt by sending ten horrendous plagues which devastated both land and people. All these signs and wonders didn't produce faith in most of the population. How can that be possible?

In the same way, we can all be under the same anointed teaching, exposed to the same ministration, and many will never enter into God's rest, (the land flowing with milk and honey). We will still find children of God perishing in the wilderness of their lives. God never denied or walked away from them, but he was unable to do for them what he had planned. They tied God's hands because of their unbelief.

All sin is rooted in unbelief. Sin is rooted in unbelief of the word of God. For example if you don't believe that God will provide for you, it may lead you to do something fraudulent to meet your needs. If we truly trust the promises of God, we won't try to do things our way.

Consider when Moses was called up to Mount Sinai for 40 days to receive the Ten Commandments. The Israelites decided he wasn't coming back to them. They concluded that God had abandoned them, and made a golden calf to worship. It is inconceivable that in less than 40 days, they forgot the presence of God which descended on the mountain before Moses went up to God. All these show that supernatural experiences will not change the heart of someone who is not genuinely hungry to know God for themselves. In verses 1 to 3, we see that God

> **Supernatural experiences will not change the heart of someone who is not genuinely hungry to know God for themselves.**

was faithful to provide Israel's needs, but they continued to grumble. Moses was one of the few that desired to know God personally. In fact, as the Bible records, "And he said unto Him, "If Thy presence go not with me, carry us not up hence." Exodus 33:15. In fact, all Moses wanted was fellowship with God.

Unlike Moses, the Israelites fell into the same snare that Satan set for Adam and Eve.

1 Corinthians 10:6 Israel set their hearts on evil things. Genesis 3:6 Eve set her eyes on eating a forbidden fruit.

1 Corinthians 10:7 Israel chose to worship idols. Genesis 3:5 Eve chose to become her own God.

1 Corinthians 10:7 Israel ate and drank in the wrong place. Genesis 3:6-7 Eve ate the fruit with Adam.

1 Corinthians 10:8 Israel tested God. Genesis 3:4, 7 Eve and Adam decided to test God by disobeying him.

In both cases, the result was death and destruction. They suffered in their body and in their soul, because of the consequences of their actions. 1 Corinthians 10:11 admonishes us to learn from them because these things were written for our instruction. When we choose to do things like them by letting unbelief breed sin in us, we will be unable to reign in life. It isn't that God takes away our crown or sonship, but we put ourselves under satanic oppression. The children of Israel never stopped being called the people of God even when they were perishing in the desert, but they still died like mere men.

Notice that all the Israelites that died in the desert during their 40 year journey, were not killed as a result of battles they fought. They died as a result of their own sins and words. Sin produces death.

Romans 8:12

"Therefore, brothers and sisters, we have an obligation—but it is not to the flesh, to live according to it. [13] For if you live according to the flesh, you will die; but if by the Spirit you put to death the misdeeds of the body, you will live."

This principle applies both in the Old and New Testament. You can, however, choose to live the abundant life God has for you through obedience to the Spirit. Choose to live under the obedience and leadership of the Spirit. He has promised to lead us into abundant pastures. Except God is your shepherd, you shall continue to want. Psalm 23:1.

In closing, am I saying that if you experience lack or the challenges of life, there is something wrong with you? No! That isn't the purpose of this book. Since we live in a fallen world, trouble and catastrophe can hit us without being of our own making, but they should not consume us. When we are in such situations, we shouldn't feel we did something wrong. Let us always remember that God within us has given us the authority to reign over troubles and come out with no smell of smoke on us.

You may also find yourself in a situation where you have lost everything for the sake of Christ. That doesn't make you poor. Poverty/wealth/health is a state of being, not about what you have. We have peace, health, riches etc. not because of our present circumstances, but because that is who we are in Christ. This is about living within that mindset, and in every situation, maintaining your confession of faith.

Prayer of Salvation

You may be someone who has never made Jesus the Lord of your life. All it takes is the simple act of believing totally in his coming and dying on the cross for your sins, and being raised from the dead after three days. If you confess with your mouth that Jesus is Lord and believe in your heart that God raised him from the dead, you shall be saved. You can pray this simple prayer:

Lord Jesus, I come to you today because I know that I am a sinner and I cannot save myself. I believe that you are God and that you came in human flesh to live and die, carrying my sins to the cross. I accept what you did on the cross for me, and today I confess you as my Lord and my Saviour. Come into my heart and change me. Make me your child. From today I want to live my life for your glory. Thank you for receiving me as your child. I am born again and my sins are washed away.

www.ingramcontent.com/pod-product-compliance
Lightning Source LLC
Chambersburg PA
CBHW071023080526
44587CB00015B/2479